Why Why Why

do astronauts float in space?

Miles Kelly

PUBLISHING

First published in 2005 by
Miles Kelly Publishing Ltd
Bardfield Centre, Great Bardfield, Essex, CM7 4SL

Copyright © Miles Kelly Publishing Ltd 2005

2 4 6 8 10 9 7 5 3 1

Editorial Director
Belinda Gallagher

Art Director
Jo Brewer

Editorial Assistant
Amanda Askew

Author
Chris Oxlade

Volume Designer
Jo Brewer

Indexer
Helen Snaith

Production Manager
Estela Boulton

Scanning and Reprographics
Anthony Cambray, Mike Coupe, Ian Paulyn

ISBN 1-84236-606-8

Printed in China

British Library Cataloguing-in-Publication Data
A catalogue record for this book is available
from the British Library

www.mileskelly.net
info@mileskelly.net

Contents

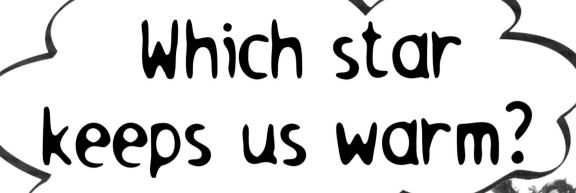

Which star keeps us warm?

The Sun does. It is a star like all the others in the night sky, but it is much closer to Earth. The Sun is a giant ball of hot, glowing gas and it gives off heat that keeps the Earth warm. It also gives us light.

Hot hot hot!

The Sun's surface is so hot that it would melt a metal spacecraft flying near it! It is 15 times hotter than boiling water.

When is it night time during the day?

Sometimes the Sun, the Earth and the Moon all line up in space. When this happens, the Moon's shadow falls on the Earth, making it dark even if it's daytime. This is called an eclipse.

Eclipse

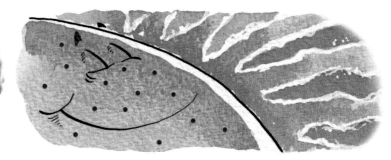

Sunspot

Why is the Sun spotty?

Some parts of the Sun's surface are cooler than the rest of it. These cooler parts appear darker than the rest of the Sun, like spots on its surface. They are called sunspots.

Remember

Never look straight at the Sun. Your eyes could be badly damaged.

Is Earth the only planet near the Sun?

There are eight other planets near the Sun. Mercury and Venus are nearer to the Sun than the Earth is. The other planets are further away. All the planets move around the Sun in huge circles. The Sun and its family of planets is called the Solar System.

Saturn

Uranus

Neptune

Pluto

Draw

Can you draw a picture of all the planets? You could copy the pictures on this page.

Do other planets have moons?

The Sun

Earth is not the only planet with a moon. Mars has two moons. Jupiter and Saturn have more than 30 moons each. Venus and Mercury are the only planets with no moons.

Mercury

The Moon

Venus

Earth

Mars

Jupiter

What are the other planets like?

Mercury, Venus and Mars are rocky planets, like the Earth. They have solid surfaces. Jupiter, Saturn, Uranus and Neptune are balls of gas and liquid. They are much bigger than the rocky planets. The last planet, Pluto, is solid and icy.

One big, happy family!

There are millions of smaller members in the Sun's family. Tiny specks of dust speed between the planets along with chunks of rock called asteroids.

What is inside the Earth?

There are layers of hot rock inside the Earth. We live on the Earth's surface where the rock is solid. Beneath the surface, the rock is hot. In some places, it has melted. This melted rock may leak from a volcano.

Crust

Mantle

Inner core

Outer core

Living it up!

Earth is the only planet with water on its surface. This means that people, plants and animals can live here. No life has yet been found on other planets.

New Moon

Crescent Moon

First quarter Moon

Gibbous Moon

Full Moon

Why does the Moon change shape?

The Sun lights up one side of the Moon. The other side is dark. As the Moon circles the Earth, we see different parts of the lit side. This is why the Moon seems to change shape.

The Moon

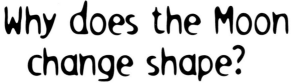

Why do we have day and night?

The Earth spins round once every day. When the part you live on faces the Sun, it is daytime. When this part faces away from the Sun, the sunlight can't reach you. Then it is night time.

Look

Look at the picture of the Moon. The circles are called craters. They were made by lumps of rock smashing into the Moon's surface.

What is the hottest planet?

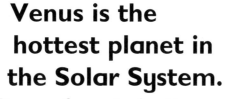

Venus is the hottest planet in the Solar System. Its surface is hotter than the inside of an oven. Venus is covered in a blanket of thick, yellow gas. The gases trap heat from the Sun but don't let it escape. This means that Venus can't cool down.

Back in a year!

Nobody has ever been to Mars. It is so far away that it would take a spacecraft six months to get there. It would take another six months to get home again!

Venus

Why is Mars called the red planet?

Mars looks red because it is covered with red rocks and red dust, the colour of rust. Sometimes, winds pick up the dust and make swirling dust storms. In 1971 dust storms covered the whole planet. The surface completely disappeared from view!

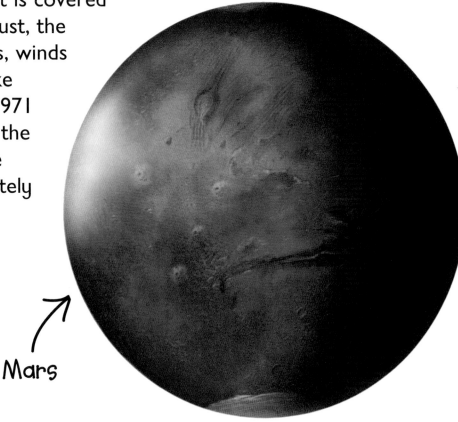

Mars

Which planet has the biggest volcano?

Mars has the biggest volcano. It is called Olympus Mons and it is three times higher than Mount Everest, the highest mountain on Earth. Olympus Mons has gently sloping sides, like an upside-down plate. Mars has many other volcanoes, too. There are also giant canyons and craters.

Discover

Try looking for Venus in the night sky. It looks like a bright star in the early morning or evening.

What is the smallest planet?

Pluto is the smallest planet in the Solar System. It is smaller than our Moon. Pluto has one moon, called Charon, which is half the size of Pluto. Because Pluto is a long way away, the Sun is just a tiny speck of light.

Charon, Pluto's moon

Pluto

Pluto's surface

Why does Mercury look like the Moon?

Mercury looks a bit like our Moon. It is covered in dents called craters. These were made when rocks crashed into the surface. There is no wind or rain on Mercury, or the Moon, to wear away the craters.

Sun trap!
Mercury is very close to the Sun. It gets much hotter there than on Earth. If you travelled to Mercury, you would need a special spacesuit and shoes to protect you from the heat.

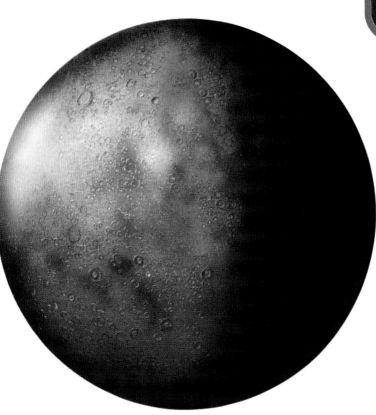

← Mercury

Think
Pluto is the coldest planet. Can you think why?

Which planet is baking hot and freezing cold?

Mercury is hot and cold. It spins very slowly. The side that faces the Sun is baked until it is hotter than the inside of an oven. When this side faces away from the Sun, it cools down until it is colder than a freezer.

What is the biggest planet?

Jupiter is the biggest planet. It is 11 times as wide as the Earth. All the other planets in the Solar System would fit inside it! Jupiter is covered in swirls of red and orange gas. These are giant storms.

Giant storm

Jupiter

Moon pizza!

Io is one of Jupiter's moons. It is covered in yellow and orange blotches. Io looks like a pizza in space! The blotches are made by hot liquid that comes out of volcanoes.

Saturn's rings →

Saturn

Which planet has rings?

Saturn is surrounded by rings that shine brightly in the sunlight. The rings are made from millions and millions of lumps of ice. Some lumps are the size of ice cubes. Others are as big as cars!

Count

Can you count how many planet Earths there are on these pages?

Is there a giant made of gas?

Not really! However, Jupiter and Saturn are called gas giants. This is because they don't have solid surfaces like the Earth. They have a thick layer of gas and then liquid. You couldn't land on them in a spacecraft.

Which planet rolls around?

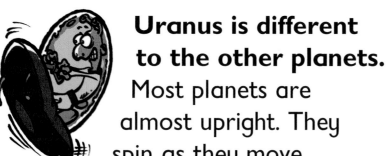

Uranus is different to the other planets. Most planets are almost upright. They spin as they move around the Sun. Uranus is tipped right over on its side. This planet spins, too, but it looks as though it is rolling around!

New new moons!

Astronomers (scientists that study space) keep finding new moons around Uranus. They have found 27 so far. There are four big moons and lots of small ones. But there may be more!

Uranus

Why does Neptune look so blue?

Neptune is covered in bright blue clouds. Sometimes there are streaky, icy white clouds, too. One white cloud is called The Scooter because it scoots around Neptune at high speed. There is also a giant storm called the Great Dark Spot.

Great Dark Spot

Neptune

Why do Neptune and Pluto swap places?

Most of the planets move around the Sun in huge circles. Pluto's circle is a bit squashed. This means that it is sometimes closer to the Sun than Neptune. Then it is Neptune's turn to be the planet that is furthest from the Sun!

Remember

Uranus and Neptune have rings. Which other two planets have rings, too?

Are there snowballs in space?

Not really! However, comets are a bit like giant snowballs. They are made up of dust and ice mixed together. When a comet gets close to the Sun, the ice begins to melt. Then dust and gas stream away from the comet. They form a long, bright tail.

What is a shooting star?

A shooting star is a bright streak across the night sky. It is not really a star. It is made when a small lump of rock shoots into the air above the Earth. Because the rock is going so fast, it burns brightly.

Comet

Asteroid
belt

Does the Sun have a belt?

The Sun has a belt made up of lumps of rock called asteroids. We call this the asteroid belt. The asteroids move around the Sun between Mars and Jupiter. The biggest asteroids are round, but most are shaped like giant potatoes.

Discover

Can you find out the name of a famous comet?

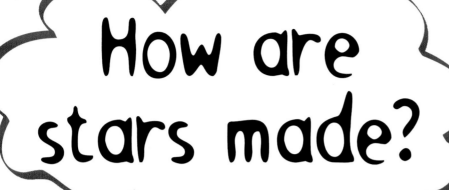

How are stars made?

1. Cloud of gas and dust

Stars are made from huge clouds of dust and gas. Gradually the cloud shrinks and all the gas and dust clump together. The centre of the cloud gets hotter and hotter and a new star begins to shine. The star gives off heat and light.

3. Star begins to shine

Shine on!

Stars can shine for thousands of millions of years! The Sun started shining five thousand million years ago. It will stop shining in another five thousand million years.

4. New star

What is a group of stars called?

A group of stars is called a star cluster. A star cluster is made from a giant cloud of gas and dust. Some clusters contain just a few stars. Others contain hundreds of stars and they look like a big ball of light.

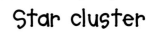

Star cluster

2. The cloud begins to spin

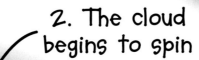

Are all stars white?

Only the most giant stars shine with a bright white light. This is because they are extremely hot. Smaller stars, such as our Sun, are not so hot. They look yellow instead. Very small stars are cooler still. They look red or brown.

Draw

Can you paint white, yellow and red stars on a sheet of black paper?

What is the Milky Way?

The stars in space are in huge groups called galaxies. Our galaxy is called the Milky Way. All the stars in the night sky are in the Milky Way. There are so many that you couldn't count them all in your whole lifetime!

Can galaxies crash?

Sometimes two galaxies crash into each other. But there is no giant bump. This is because galaxies are mostly made of empty space! The stars just go past each other. Galaxies can pull each other out of shape.

Count

Look at the pictures on these pages. How many different shapes of galaxies can you find?

The Milky Way

Elliptical galaxy

Irregular galaxy

Spiral galaxy

Do galaxies have arms?

Some galaxies have arms that curl in a spiral, like the Milky Way. Other galaxies, called elliptical galaxies, have a round, squashed shape. Many galaxies have no shape and are called irregular galaxies.

Great galaxies!

There are thousands of millions of galaxies in space. Some are much smaller than the Milky Way. Others are much larger. They all contain too many stars to count!

How does a shuttle get into space?

Booster rocket

Tower

A shuttle blasts into space like a big rocket. It has rocket motors in its tail. They get fuel from a giant fuel tank. There are two booster rockets, too. The fuel tank and the booster rockets fall off before the shuttle reaches space.

USA

Rocket power!
Rockets are filled with fuel. The fuel burns in the rocket motor to make hot gases. The gases rush out of the motor and push the rocket upwards.

Fuel
tank

How fast do rockets go?

Very, very fast indeed! After blasting off, a rocket goes faster and faster and higher and higher. When it reaches space, it is going 30 times faster than a jumbo jet. If a rocket went slower than this it would fall back to Earth.

Rocket

Space
shuttle

Make

Blow up a balloon and then let it go. The air rushes out and pushes the balloon along, like a simple rocket.

Rocket
motors

When is a shuttle like a glider?

When a shuttle travels back to Earth it slows down. Then it begins to fall. It does not use its motors to fly down. Instead, it flies like a giant glider. The shuttle lands on a long runway and uses a parachute to slow to a stop.

Why do astronauts float in space?

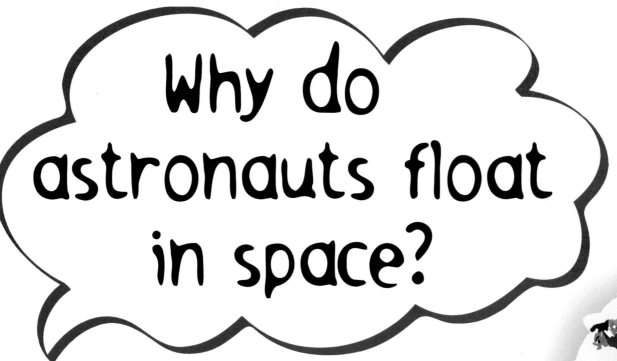

When things are in space they don't have any weight. This means everything floats. So do astronauts! This makes them feel sick, too. In a spacecraft everything is fixed down to stop it floating away. Astronauts have footholds and handholds to grab onto.

All packed?

Astronauts must take everything they need into space. In space there is no air, water or food. All of these things have to be packed into the spacecraft and taken into space.

Astronaut

Sleeping bag

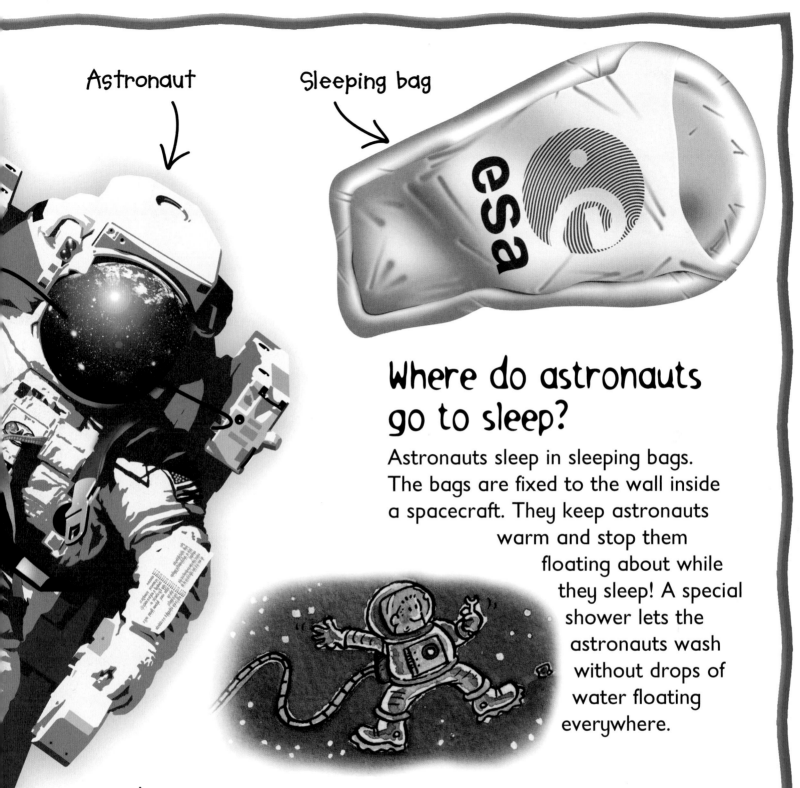

Where do astronauts go to sleep?

Astronauts sleep in sleeping bags. The bags are fixed to the wall inside a spacecraft. They keep astronauts warm and stop them floating about while they sleep! A special shower lets the astronauts wash without drops of water floating everywhere.

Why do astronauts wear spacesuits?

Space is a dangerous place. Spacesuits protect astronauts when they go outside their spacecraft. There is no air in space. So a spacesuit has a supply of air for the astronaut to breathe. The suit also stops an astronaut from getting too hot or too cold.

Remember

Can you remember why astronauts have to carry air with them in space?

Are there robots in space?

There are robot spacecraft, called probes, in space. They have visited all the planets, except Pluto. Some probes travel around the planets. They send photographs and other information back to Earth. Other probes land on a planet to take a closer look.

Snap happy!
A probe called *Voyager 2* was the first to visit Uranus and Neptune.
It took photographs of the planets and sent them back to Earth.

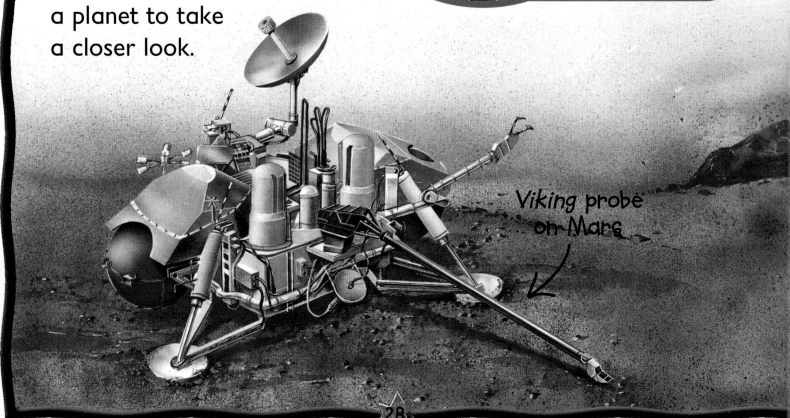

Viking probe on Mars

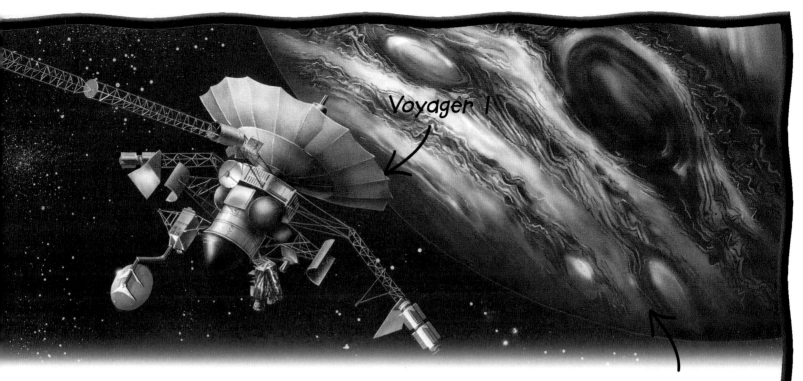

Voyager 1

Jupiter

Which probe has travelled the furthest?

A probe called *Voyager 1* was launched from Earth in 1977. It visited Jupiter in 1979 and then Saturn in 1980. Then it kept going, out of the Solar System. *Voyager 1* is now 14 thousand million kilometres from Earth!

Draw

Try designing your own robot explorer. You can take some ideas from these pages.

Sojourner

Have probes been to Mars?

More probes have been to Mars than any other planet. In 1997 a probe called Pathfinder landed on Mars. Inside Pathfinder was a tiny robot vehicle, called *Sojourner*. Scientists steered it using remote control. It investigated the soil and rocks on Mars.

Quiz time

Do you remember what you have read about space? Here are some questions to test your memory. The pictures will help you. If you get stuck, read the pages again.

1. Which star keeps us warm?

page 4

2. Why is the Sun spotty?

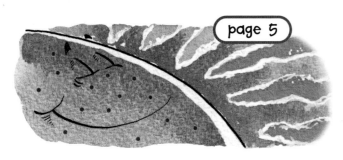

page 5

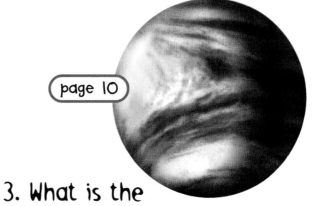

page 10

3. What is the hottest planet?

4. Why is Mars called the red planet?

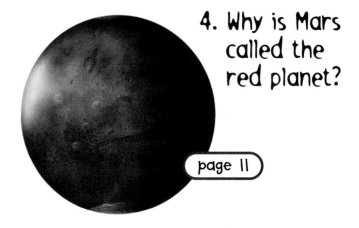

page 11

page 12

5. What is the smallest planet?

page 18

6. What is a shooting star?

7. Does the Sun have a belt?

page 19

8. What is a group of stars called?

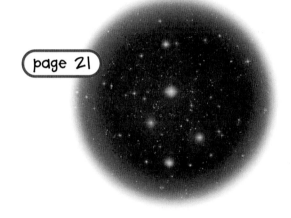

page 21

9. What is the Milky Way?

page 22

10. Can galaxies crash?

page 22

11. How does a shuttle get into space?

page 24

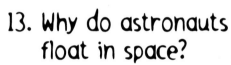

12. When is a shuttle like a glider?

page 25

13. Why do astronauts float in space?

page 26

Answers

1. The Sun.
2. Cooler parts look darker, like spots.
3. Venus.
4. It is covered with red rocks and dust.
5. Pluto.
6. A lumpof rock burning in the sky.
7. Yes, the asteroid belt.
8. Star cluster.
9. A huge group of stars.
10. Yep.
11. Like a giant rocket does.
12. When it travels back to Earth.
13. Because they have no weight in space.

Index